Richard Allestree

The Divine Autority and Usefulness of the Holy Scripture

asserted in a sermon on the 2 Timothy 3. 15

Richard Allestree

The Divine Autority and Usefulness of the Holy Scripture
asserted in a sermon on the 2 Timothy 3. 15

ISBN/EAN: 9783337780678

Printed in Europe, USA, Canada, Australia, Japan

Cover: Foto ©Lupo / pixelio.de

More available books at **www.hansebooks.com**

THE

Divine Autority

AND

USEFULNESS

OF THE

Holy Scripture

ASSERTED IN A

SERMON

On the 2 *Timothy* 3. 15.

By *R. ALLESTREE D. D.*
and Chaplain in Ordinary to his Majesty.

OXFORD
At the THEATER. 1673.

2. Tim. 3. 15.

*And that from a child thou haſt known the holy
Scriptures, which are able to make thee wiſe
unto ſalvation, through faith which is in
Chriſt Jeſus.*

THE words are part of St. *Pauls* reaſon-
ing, by which he preſſeth *Timothy* to hold
faſt the truth he had receiv'd, and not let
evil men, ſeducers, work him out of what he had
bin taught : urging to this end both the auterity
of the Teacher, himſelf, who had ſecur'd the truth
of his doctrine by infallible evidence ; and beyond that, as if that were a more effectual enforce-
ment, preſſing him with his own education in the
Scriptures ; how he had bin nurſt up in that faith,
ſuckt the Religion with his milk, that it was grown
the very habit of his mind, that which would
ſtrengthen him into a perfect man in Chriſt, and
make

make him *wife unto falvation* if he did continue in the faith and practife of it ; which he proves in the remaining verfes of the Chapter.

In the words read there are three things obfervable.

1. Here is a ftate fuppos'd , *Salvation* ; and put too as of fuch concernment , that attaining it is lookt upon as wifdom ; *wife unto falvation.*

Now fince true wifdom muft exprefs it felf both in the end that it propofeth , and the means it choofeth for that end to be purfued with and attain'd by , and take care both thefe have all conditions that can juftify the undertaking , and fecure the prudence of it , and this wifdom to falvation therefore muft fuppofe both thefe; in order to them both we have here

2. That which with all divine advantage does propofe this end , and alfo does prefcribe moft perfect means for the attaining it ; and that is *Holy Scripture through faith which is in Chrift Jefus. Thou haft known the holy Scriptures which are able to make thee wife unto falvation, through faith which is in Chrift Jefus.* Holy Scripture probably of the Old Teftament ; for there was hardly any other *Timothy* could know from a child, fcarce any other being

ing

ing written then. The faith of that then through
the *faith which is in Chrift Jefus*, that is, together
with the faith of all things neceffary to be known
concerning Chrift, is meant. Now fince St. *John*,
after the view of all that the other three Evangelifts
had wrote concerning Chrift, adding his ftory al-
fo fays, that Chrift * *did and fpoke more then what* * John 20. 30,
is written, yet affirms moft pofitively that *thofe* 31.
*things were written that we might believe that Jefus
is the Chrift, the Son of God, and believing might have
life through his name* ; and fo enough is written for
that faith which is in Jefus that is neceffary to eternal life : therefore the Holy Scripture of the Old
Teftament, together with the faith of what is written in the New, is that which St. *Paul* affirms is
able to make us wife unto falvation.

3. Here is the advantage *Timothy* had above o-
thers as to Faith in thefe, and confequently the far
greater obligation to continue in it. *He had known
them from a child. And that from a child thou haft
known the holy Scripture, &c.*

The firft thing that does offer it felf to our con-
fideration is the ftate fuppos'd, *Salvation.* But
becaufe my Text fuppofes it, I fhall do fo too, nor
fhall think it needful to prove here, that there is

such a state, nor consequently that all those are
stupid, who propose not to themselves this ever-
lasting safety for their main end , and by strict
care in the duties of Religion and Gods service
aime at it : for if that state be granted, nay if it
be but possible , it must be granted that there can
be no security but in doing so, nor consequently
any wisdom without being *wise* thus *unto salvation*.

But then if this were granted , that the wisest
thing man could propose to himself, were by strict
care in all the duties of Religion to design Gods
honor and his own salvation ; still , as to the o-
ther part of prudence which consists in the choice
of means , we are to seek for that Religion
we are to pursue this end by and attain it ;
since there are so many and so opposite Reli-
gions in the word , that 'tis not easier to recon-
cile them , then to make peace betwixt enemies and
contradictions. And it alwaies was so ; for ex-
cepting that mankind agree'd still in the notion of
the necessity of Religion , that all had apprehen-
sions of invisible powers above us , and differ'd
not much in the rules of Justice and Morality , in
other things there was no nearness. Almost from
the beginning there was more variety of Gods then
Nations

Nations, I had almoft faid then Worfhippers. Beafts·
were their Sacrifices and their Deities, and therefore the votaries were certainly no better. Vices
alfo were their worfhips; things which their Cities and their Camps would not endure, found
Sanctuary in their Temples; and the actions which
were whipt in the Judgment-hall, were their piety in the holy places. And tho· fome wife men
among them found good reafon to decry this, yet
they knew not what to take up in the ftead. I need
not add the prefent differences of the world, even
that call'd Chriftian too, great part of which as
heretofore they feal'd their faith with their own
blood, now feal it in the blood of all that differ
from them; and by their perfecutions hope to me-
rit Heaven more, then thofe did hope to gain it by
their Martyrdoms. But thefe I need not add to
make up this into a demonftration, that it is impoffible for lapfed men, fo far as they are left to themfelves, and have no other guide to follow but their
reafon, to find out what they are to believe of
God, and how to ferve him, and fave themfelves.
The a *Fathers* and b *Philofophers* too, conclude that
we can learn from none but God, what we muft underftand of God; who muft be known only as he
himfelf

a *Hil.l.*1*.de Tri-
nit. p.*53,54·
C'emens Al.
Strom. 6.p.675.
εἴπερ ὂν κỳ κρατά
b Πλάτωνα ἢ πα-
ρὰ ϑ Θιᶙ, ἤπειρϼ
τῶν ἀκρϼων ϑ
Θιᶙ τὸ ἀληϑὶς
ἀκμανϑάνειν
μϓϖς οἴοντι,
εἰκότως πυερϼ,
τῶν ϑείων λογί-
ον τὰ μϼενϽελα
ἐκλεγϼμενοι τλὼ
ἀλήϑειαν αυχϼ-
μιν ἐκδιδάσκιοϽ
διὰ ϑ γ̔ὖ Θιᶙ.
Vid. Juftin.
Mart. ad Diog-
netum p.499.A-
thanas. ad Se-
rapioncm tom. 1.
p. 191. 194.
edit. Par. 1673.

B 3

himfelf is pleas'd to revele himfelf. His worfhip
alfo, how he will be ferv'd, and what obfervances
he does require, or will admit, fince it depends on
his own good plefure, therefore without his di-
rections 'tis in vain to hope to pleafe him with
our Religious fervice whatever it be, and by confequence impoffible without his guidance and af-
fiftance to acquire the end of all our Service and
Religion, *the falvation of our fouls*. So that how wife
foever he be who does propofe this bleffed end to
himfelf, if yet withall he be not fome way from
the Lord inftructed by what means he muft pur-
fue that end, and do not make choice of, and ufe
thofe means, it is impoffible he can be *wife unto*
falvation. Now for this St. *Paul* affures us moft
exprefly, here we may be furnifhed: For he faies,
The Holy Scriptures are able to make us wife unto fal-
vation, through faith which is in Chrift Jefus.
And he does affert this on the very ground we
mention'd, for they are Θεόπνευσαι, infpir'd by
God; they come from him. All which muft be
made out in the next place.

That thofe Holy Scriptures which St. *Paul* firft
mentions, thofe of the Old Teftament were fo, and
did contain fufficient revelation both of God, and
of

of the way of worſhip of the Jews, that Nation did ſo perfectly believe, that neither Sufferings nor Miracles could perſwade the contrary; neither the Roman perſecuters that deſtroy'd their worſhip, nor the Son of God that chang'd it, could yet take them off from *Moſes* and his Scriptures. Now that this *Moſes* led that Nation out of *Egypt* with an high hand, and made himſelf their Prince and Law-giver, multitudes of [a] forreign Hiſtories of the firſt times, and the beſt account aſſure us: whoſe relations we cannot queſtion as deriv'd from themſelves, becauſe they hated Jews beyond all poſſibility of ſuch compliance. But the [b] Scriptures alſo tell us, how in *Egypt* by ſtrange wonders, (ſuch as their Magicians could not imitate nor bear, who tho they had permiſſion to do ſome, it was that ſo they might appear to be outdon the more miraculouſly, themſelves confeſſing Gods hand in thoſe prodigies) *Moſes* wrought on the *Egyptians* to give leave the people ſhould depart: and how when yet notwithſtanding that leave given they were purſu'd, he made way for them through the [c] Sea by Miracles, which was a rampart and defence to them, a ruine to their enemies: How they were [d] fed for forty years with Manna raining down from Heaven

[a] *Juſtin. ex Trogo. l. 36. Diod. Sicul. l. 1. Strabo l. 16. Plinius 30. Tacitus Hiſt. 5. Joſeph. contra Apionem mentions many others.*

[b] Exod. 7, 8, 9, 10. Chapters.

[c] Exod. 14. 21.

[d] Exod. 16. 15. Deut. 8. 24.

Heaven in the wildernefs : and that they might
depend on Providence for their daily provifion,
when he forbad them to take care or gather for the
morrow , whatfoe're their greedinefs or want of
faith provided,ftrait bred, worms and ftank, except that on the Sabbath eve, to keep off fuch cares
from the day of their Religion, they gather'd dou-
ble which b corrupted not : How when they muti-
ned for flefh , would have variety , Paradife in the
defert , fuch great plenty of c Quailes flew to them
as fed the whole Nation till their very luft was fur-
fetted ; and they had no more will then hunger
to them : How *Mofes* Rod did ftrike a living ftream,
a River that fuffic'd that people and their cattle out
of a d Rock : How in the midft of lightning and
thunder God himfelf promulgated his Law e to the
whole Nation audibly at once : How his glorious
prefence fhew'd it felf in all neceffities upon the
Ark,in which the Tables of the Law were laid up :
How the waters of the river f *Jordan* fled from that
Ark both waies, flow'd upwards to give paffage
to the people into *Canaan* : How the walls of g *Je-*
richo without any other battery, any other force
but that the Ark was there, fell down before it.

But to name no more, If thefe be true ; that
power

*Exod. 16.20.

' Exod. 16.24

c Num. 11. 19,
20, 31, 32.

d Num. 20. 8.
11.

e Exod. 20.

f Josh. 3. 16.

g Josh. 6. 20.

power by which thefe were wrought, was great
enough to give that Law, require obedience to it,
and reward it, and to punifh all tranfgreffion according to the tenor of thefe Scriptures: that is,
it was God; and he that wrote thofe Scriptures
muft have had communication with, and bin infpir'd from, God to write them. But,

2. Whether they were true or no according as
they are recorded in thofe Scriptures, that whole
people from the greateft almoft to the leaft muft
know; becaufe they are recorded as all don, not
only in the prefence of them all, but as the objects and the entertainments of their fenfes, every
one; fo that if they were forg'd, not one of the
whole Nation could be ignorant of it. And then,

3. If they knew them forg'd all; that [a] 600000
men, befides their wives and families, fhould endure this *Mofes*, having brought them forth only
into a wildernefs, there to lay fuch a heavy Law,
and fo fevere a yoke upon them, with fuch penal-
ties annext to every leaft tranfgreffion, and adjure
them to obferve it on the account of all thofe prodigies that had bin wrought among them, and
upbraid them with ftiffneckednefs, rebellion, and
appeal to their own fenfes for the truth of all this,

[a] Num. 2. 32.
Num. 11. 21.

C   and

and record all to pofterity in this Scripture, caufe
all to be read before them ; and that they fhould
bear all this from him they knew fo impudent a de-
ceiver, and conveigh that Scripture and the faith
of it to their pofterity, ground their fo ftrict, fo
chargeable Religion on that book, which they were
certain had no word of truth in it : this fure tran-
fcends belief and poffibility.

'Tis certain therefore, fince the Jews of that
age did perform the fervices requir'd, and in per-
forming them according as that book directs, did
teach their children the great works that God had
don in their fight, therefore they believ'd thofe Miracles and Scriptures. And fince it was impoffible
that they fhould be deceiv'd; if they believ'd them,
they were true : and their pofterity receiv'd from
them the faith of this, and fo deriv'd it on, that
neither Gods dread judgments, nor mans cruelty
can yet fhake it. Now had they not bin don, and on
that account conveigh'd; when ever they were
broacht, and that book firft appear'd, the men of
that age muft needs know their Fathers never had
perform'd fuch fervices, had fuch a book read to
them conftantly, nor told them of fuch Miracles
that had bin wrought: and therefore 'twas impoffible

poffible that they could have believ'd it had bin fo
from *Mofes*, if it had bin true that it had firft be-
gun to be taught in their own time, or in theirs
with whom they liv'd. And this difcourfe muft be
of force concerning every age, if we afcend until
we come to that of *Mofes* wherein all was effected.
Yet befides this, they had alfo that perpetual Miracle in the High Prieft's Pectoral, the Oracle of *Vrim*
and *Thummim*, that did keep alive their faith and
ftrengthen it: and they had Prophets conftantly
foretelling, as from God, things that were fomtimes
fuddenly to come to pafs, and fomtimes not till
many ages after, the event of which depended often on the will of thofe that would not of fome
hundred years be born; others on Gods own im-
mediat will and hand: and therefore none but
God could look into, foretel, and bring to pafs all
thofe events. Now fuch were *Jeremies* predictions
of the taking of *Jerufalem*, and the captivity of the
people, and the exprefs number of [a] years it would [a] Jer. 25. 11. 12
continue; *Efays* naming [b] *Cyrus*, who was to releafe [b] Ifa 44. 26. 21.
it, near two hundred years e're he was born; All   28. & 45. 1.
Daniels prophecies, particularly that moft eminent
one of the [c] *Meffiah* this *Chrift Jefus*, of whofe Scri- [c] Dan. 9. 24.
ptures we are next to fpeak.   &c.

That that *Jesus*, whom *Cornelius Tacitus*
the heathen historian in the fifteenth book
of his Annals, calls *Christiani dogmatis auto-
rem*, the [a] Author of the Christian Doctrine,
did work Miracles, and prophesy, both [b] Jews
and learned [c] Heathens do confess. But these
Books tell us, when he first began to preach,
he publicly cast out a Devil in the Synagogue on
the Sabbath day; and at even, when the whole
City was assembled, he heal'd all their sick, and
cast out many Devils, which confest before all, that
he was the Son of [d] God. Then he cast out a Legion of
such mischievous malign Spirits, as having got li-
cense, drove two thousand Swine headlong into the
Sea & choakt them, which was known to the whole
Country of the [e] *Gadarens.* Before the Pharisees
and Doctors, that came out of all the Cities both
of *Galilee,* and *Jewry,* and *Jerusalem,* and so great a
crowd as forc'd them to unroof the house to come
to him, he freed one from his [f] palsy and his sins.
A multitude was witness of the death of [g] *Jairus's*
daughter, and bewailing her laught him to scorn
that undertook to raise her, yet he call'd her into
life. And on a feast day in the Temple, before all
the

[a] *Tac. An. l.* 15.

[b] *Vid. Raim. Martin. pug. fid. p.* 2. *c.* 8.
[c] *Celsus apud Orig. l.* 2. *Julian. Cyril. contra ipsum* 6. *Origen. contra Cel. l.* 2. *c.* 69.

[d] *Mat.* 8. *Mar.* 1. *Luc.* 4.

[e] *Mat.* 8. *Mar.* 5. *Luc.* 8.

[f] *Mat.* 9. *Mar.* 2. *Luc.* 5.

[g] *Mar.* 5. *Luc.* 8.

the people, he recover'd one that had lain lame
[b] eight and thirty years : and when a widows fon [b] John 5.
was carried to his funeral, and all the City follow'd
him, he only toucht the bier , and bid him [c] live. [c] Luc. 7.
With two fifhes and five loaves he fed [d] 5000 men [d] Mat. 14.
befides women and children , and with what they Mar. 6.
Luc. 9.
left they fill'd twelve baskets, when one basket car- Joh. 6.
ried all before they ate ; fo that they were convinc'd , he was that Prophet that was to come into
the world : and with feven loaves he fill'd [e] 4000 [e] Mat. 15.
Mar. 8.
afterwards and feven baskets. He comman-
ded a dumb fpirit out of him that had bin [f] Luna- [f] Mat. 17.
Mar. 9.
tic , vext with a Devil from his infancy,before the Luc. 9.
people and the Scribes , whom his Difciples could
not caft out. And when [g] *Lazarus* had bin dead [g] John 11.
four daies, and buried till he ftank , yet at his call,
altho bound hand and foot with grave cloaths ,
he came forth,all the multitude beholding. From
fo many more I chofe out thefe,becaufe they are re-
ported don before the people,and the Scribes, and
Pharifees,and Doctors. I might name his [a] Prophe- [a] Mat. 24.
Mar. 13.
cies of the deftruction of Jerufalem,and of the pro- Luc. 21.
pagation and continuance of his Religion;even of
the womans box of [b] Spikenard, which event hath [b] Mat. 26.
made Mar. 14.
John 12.

made notorious to the world. But his death
was fo even at the prefent : when if the rending
of the ^c veil of the temple was apparent Miracle

made notorious to the world. But his death
was fo even at the prefent : when if the rending
of the ᶜ veil of the temple was apparent Miracle
to all Jerufalem, the funs prodigious Eclips, when
it was impoffible by nature he fhould be eclips'd
(it being then full moon,) was fo to the whole
Hemifphere. It ferves the ufe I am to make of this,
that 'tis here recorded, but withall Heathen ᵈ Hiftorians and Chronologers bear witnefs to it: for
when they relate that in the 4ᵗʰ year of the 202
Olympiad, the year that is affign'd to Chrift's
death, there was fuch a great Eclipfe as never
had bin, day at noon turn'd into night, the ftars
appearing, and earthquakes as far as Bythynia,
fince 'tis apparent by the motions of the Heavens
and the calculations of Aftronomy, there could be
none fuch then according to the courfe of nature,
it muft be this the Gofpel fpeaks of. But beyond
all this, 'tis regiftred here, that according as he had
foretold, he rais'd himfelf from death the ᵃ 3ᵈ day;
yea and many bodies of the Saints that had bin
buried, long it may be fome of them, he rais'd
with him. That notwithftanding all the art and
treachery of the Cheif Priefts to conceal it, yet
that very day he appear'd ᵇ Firft to Mary Magd-
dalen,

ᶜ Mat. 27.
Mar. 15.
Luc. 23.
John. 19.

*Phlegon apud O-
rig: contra Cels.
l 2. p. 80. Eufeb.
ad Olym.* 202
*cnn. 4 Philip. &
Georg. Syncel.
Thallus apud A-
frican. vid. Seal.
animad. ad
Eufeb. Chron. p.*
186. *ad ann.*
2044. *Etiam
vide Juft. Mart.
p. 76. & p.* 84
*& Tertull. A-
pol. c. 21. & de
ifto terræ motu
agere Tacitum
& Plin. l. 2. c.*
84 *fcribit Oros.*

, Mat. 28 Mar.
16. Luc. 29.
John. 24.

Mar. 16. 9.

dalen, [a] 2dly the Women, 3[dly,b] Peter, 4[thly] to them
that went to [c] Emaus, laft of all on that day to the
Eleven [d] except Thomas, being feen and handled
by and eating with them; 6[thly] eight daies after
to the fame eleven with [e] Thomas; 7[thly] at the
fea of [f] Galilee appearing in a miracle of fifhes;
8[thly] to all his Difciples and [g] 500 Brethren more
in Galilee, then to James, [h] then to all his Apoftles, promifing them the [i] Holy Ghoft; and laft-
ly all of them beholding he [k] afcended into Heaven, and ten daies after as he promifed fent the [l] Holy Ghoft upon them in the fhape of fiery tongues,
fo as that they fpoke all Languages immediatly, to
the amazement of the Jews of every Nation under Heaven to which they were fcatter'd, that
the Miracle might fpread as far.

Now if all this be true, he that did thefe muft
have communication with a power above all that
we account the powers of Nature; fuch an one
moft certainly as can perform whatfoever he in
this book promifes, inflict what e're he threatens;
fuch as is divine. And fince he wrought all thefe,
on purpofe to evince he came commiffion'd from
that divine power, brought thefe Miracles as feals
of that commiffion, that we might believe him, therfore

[a] Luc. 24. 5.
[b] V. 33.
[c] V. 13.
[d] V. 36. 37. 41.
[e] John 20. 24.
[f] John 21.
[g] Mat. 28. 16. Mar. 15. 6.
[h] 1 Cor. 15. 7.
[i] Luc. 24. 49.
Act. 1. 4. 5.
[k] Act. 1. 9.
[l] Luc. 24. 51.
Act. 2. 6. 7. 8.

fore whatfoever he delivers muft be embrac't by
us, as we hope for thofe bleffed rewards that he
propofeth, and on pain of thofe eternal torments
if we do not ; of both which it is not poffible to
doubt if thefe accounts be true.

2dly Since the moft and greateft of thefe muft
be don but once ; he could not be incarnated, and
born, and live, and preach, and dye, and rife again,
and go to Heaven every day, of every age, in every
place, to convince every man by his own fenfes ;
to all thofe that did not fee the matter of fact, therefore faith of all thefe muft be made by witneffes.
And

3dly If we can be fure the witneffes that do affert a fact underftand it exactly , if the things be
palpable, and they muft certainly know whether
they were really don or no ; and if we can be
fure too, that they are fincere, will not affirm that
which they do not know , and do not lye, their
teftimony of it muft be moft infallible : becaufe it
is impoffible fuch witneffes can be deceiv'd, or will
deceive.

4^thly The witneffes in this cafe, the Apoftles and
the 70 Difciples (for I'le name no more) muft
needs know moft perfectly: For they not only faw
the

the Miracles, but were [a] inftruments and parties in fome of them ; fent to cure difeafes, caft out Devils, and knew whether all this were in earneft. And moft certainly they faw (as all the Jews did too) Chrift crucified, his heart peirc't with a fpear, and his body buried ; and whether they did fee him rifen, handle him, and eat with him they knew. And if they might miftake in his Afcenfion, yet the fiery tongues, if fuch did light on them, they muft needs fee; and whether they themfelves, who fpoke no Languages, could then fpeak Tongues, it cannot be but they muft know. In thefe there is no poffibility they could err, unlefs they did it wilfully : but then 'tis as impoffible that they could do it willfully, if they were fincere and honeft, fuch as would not lye.

Now that they were fuch, I might urge their fimplicity and opennefs, without difguife, not covering their own errors ; men who feem'd to live as well as preach againft all artifice, and to have no defign on any thing but the amendment and falvation of mankind. For he that can fuppofe it poffible that they were otherwife, men of art and finefs, that they contriv'd the ftory, muft needs know; Firft, that fuch would not feal

D their

their falfehood with their blood; defign no recom-
penfe to all their travels but contemt, and
hatred, perfecutions, prifons, whippings,
wounds and death, to be the fcum and the off-
fcouring the world; lay out their lives againft their
confcience to preach that *Jefus*, who did only
call them out to be a ª *fpectacle to all the world*,
juft fuch as Malefactors when expos'd to fight with,
and to be devour'd of wild beafts. Their fuffer-
ings are too known to ftay upon : S.ͭ *Pauls* own
catalogue of his for five whole verfes 2 *Cor.* 11.
is fuch, that to fuftain them only for this end, to
put a cheat on mankind; count a fo labori-
ous, vext, torn, miferable life and an in-
famous death gain, fo the fable might be beleiv'd:
to think they could do this, is fure as great a
madnefs as to do it. But yet I will fuppofe that
poffible; that thofe who wove the fable pleas'd
themfelves fo infinitely with the expectations of im-
pofing on mankind, as that thofe hopes could make
mifery and death it felf look lovely to them. But
Then 2.ᵈˡʸ that all and every of them fhould be
of that mind, that amongft fo many that bare
witnefs of Chrifts Miracles and refurrection not
a man fhould difcover the cheat; that when their
perfecutors

perfecutors did with arts of torment as it were examin them upon the rack, they fhould work not one fingle confeffion out of them ; that no ones courage fhould be broke, nor have a qualm fo far as to acknowledg how it was, difclofe the plot, lay open the confederacy, the whole myftery and the contrivance of it : When of twelve Difciples one was fo falfe to betray his Mafters perfon at a vile rate, yet that all of them, and many more, in a feign'd ftory of his Miracles fhould be fo true to one another, that no engin of mans cruelty even could fcrew out the fecret, not one fhould betray the forgery and be a *Judas* where he ought to be : no not that *Judas*, whofe concern it was, whofe treafon to his Mafter had bin juftified had he bin an impoftor : yet that he fhould ftir no leaft fufpicion of it, but fhould burft, choakt with his greif becaufe he had betray'd innocent blood: This, if he knew it had all bin impofture, muft be moft ftupendous.

But yet we will give them this too, that vainglorious hopes of drawing in the world to follow them, might make all of them obftinate in feorefy againft all attemts of cruelty ; or if fome

weak

weak brethren did perchance difcover, we may not have heard of it. But

For them 3dly to begin their preaching at *Jeru-falem* is yet more ftrange. To hope to draw men into a perfwafion, and to bottom that perfwafion upon Miracles, and a refurrection don a-mongft them there, where if difcovery were made it muft be made, and where it could not but be made if there were fraud. For to relate and write thofe works with every circumftance of perfons, place, and time, where they not only could examin every circumftance, but where they rather then their lives would find them falfe, if nothing elfe would, this muft needs difcover it. They preach them to the face of the whole multitude and of the *Pharifees*, and tell them they were don before their eyes, fomtimes 5.00 and fomtimes 5.000 being by and the *cheif Preifts* and *Pharifees* and *Doctors* : fo that 'twas moft impoffible they fhould not know if they were true or falfe, as fure as there was never a Jew in all the Land, but knew whether there were a darknefs over all the land when Chrift was crucified. Now if thefe were forg'd to hope to draw *Jews* out of their Religion with apparent forgeries, which

they

they knew fuch, fpeaks thefe Apoftles men fo
far from art to manage a defign of changing the
Religion of the world, that they were mad beyond recovery and prefident.

But let us give them that too. Yet tis certain
4[thly] that the Jews, if any fuch were wrought on
by them, muft be much more ftupid to believe them
upon the account of fuch things don in all the
country, in their Cities, and the Temple, before all the Nation, when they could not choofe
but know they were not don, if they were not
don, but were fain'd all. For what ever might
be motive to Chrifts followers and his Apoftles,
with the certain danger of their lives to forge
the cheat, what poffible temtation could there
be fo great to incline *Jewes*, the moft ftiffnecked
people, the moft ftubborn in Religion in the
world, to embrace a faith which nothing but the
Crofs and fhame and mifery attended, and which
they muft know falfe too ? Had they fo great luft
to dye, as for that to bid farewel to their *Mofes*,
their Religion and their Law ? It is impoffible had
they not known the truth of thofe things, that
in waters of affliction, in Jerufalem, *ipfis perfe-
cutionum fontibus*, in that fountain, that fpringhead,

of

of perfecutions, as the Fathers call it, they would ever have bin baptiz'd into Chrift.

'Yet fuddenly in one day at one fermon of St *Peter* we read near 3000 were baptiz'd. *Act.* 2. at another ftrait 5000 *Act.* 4. and fuch beginnings, fuch fums are requir'd to make good what the Governor of Paleftine.[a] *Tiberianus* tells the Emperor, that he was not fufficient to put to death all thofe that confeft themfelves Chriftians. All which muft needs have either bin convinc't thofe things were true, or elfe as well againft their confcience as againft the powers, thus embrac't that faith and death together.

In the left margin: ὡς ἐκ ἐπαρχῆ λοιπὸν τὸς χριστιανὸς φονεύειν. Suidas in voce Τεϱιανὸς.

Neither was this a firft furprize of Chriftianity, as it had feiz'd mens minds at unawares; for it went on conquering till the world came into it, receiving the Religion with the lofs of all that was dear to them in this world. For in one age from Chrifts death, what with the Apoftles fermons, miracles, and [a] writings alfo to confirm and keep men in the truth, and to conveigh it better to pofterity,

In the left margin: Whence Eufeb. fays. l. 2. Ecc. hift. c. 14. they at Rome not thinking it enough to

have heard the gofpel once μὴ δ᾽ τῇ ἀγράφῳ τ̃ θείᾳ κηρύγμαῷ διδασκαλίᾳ, not being contented with the preaching of the heavenly doctrine, while it was but an unwritten doctrine, earneftly entreat St Mark, that he would leave in writing with them a monument of that doctrine which had bin delivered to them by preaching. Nor did they give over till they had prevail'd; which when St Peter knew by revelation of the H: G. ἡσθῆναι τῇ τ̃ ἀνδρῶν προθυμίᾳ being extremly pleas'd with that defire and their earneftnefs in it, He approv'd, it and appointed it to be read in their affembly.

and

and their difciples after them, who went forth
[b] delivering thofe writings, preaching on, and *Eufeb.l.3.c.37.*
doing wonders alfo, very many Nations are recor-
ded by Hiftorians as converted almoft wholly.
And the truth of it is evident, fince nothing but
almoft whole Nations, nor yet they but as buoy'd
up by the wonders and the graces of Cods fpirit,
ever could be able to endure, or be fufficient to
employ the Swords, the Flames, the Lions, and
the other numberlefs tortures which the *Jews* and
Nero and *Domitian*, and above all *Trajan* in that firft
age rag'd with, till they made their Cities, vil-
lages and provinces fo defolate,that the Proconful
Pliny, being frighted with the multitude of mur-
der'd Chriftians, did advife with him about re-
laxing his edicts, as he himfelf [a] affures us.   *l. 10.epift. 97.*

It was the fame the next age, when the power
of Miracles [b] yet liv'd, and thofe which Chrift *Juft.Mart.dial.*
himfelf wrought were fcarce all dead, (fome [c] liv'd *cum Tryph. Ju-*
till near that time, who rofe up with him at his *de e p.247. 302.*
refurrection;) when thefe[d] books, (writ by the will *311.Iren. l. 2. c.*
of God to be the pillar and foundation of mens *56. 57.*
faith in after ages, as faith [e] *Irenæus* in that age,) *puid Euf. l. 4. c. 3.*
were alfo read in the affemblies weekly; when *Pol.2.p. 98.*
not only thofe that did affemble were by [f] Ha-   *e Iren.l. 3. c. 1.*
                                                    drian

f *Juſt. Mar. A-*
pol. 2. Eccl.
Smyrnens. apud
Euſeb. l.4.c.15.
Eccleſiarum Vi-
ennen. & Lug.
dun. comment.
de paſſione Mar-
tyr. ſuorum a-
pud Euſeb.l.5.c.
1.& Niceph.
l.3. & 4.
g *Orig cont.Cel*
l.2. p. 62. & p.
80. Tertul. A-
pol c.23.
h *Niceph. l.5.*
c. 29.
V.Euſeb.l.6.&
7.ferè integros.
de ʃ 2. Sparti-
an.& Tertul.
de Decio S.Cypr.
b *Euſeb. l.8.c.2.*
c.6.Niceph.l. 7.
c.6.Euſeb.l.8 c.
11.&c.9. Sulp.
Sev.l.2. Oros.l.
7.c. 25. Ignatii
Patr.Antioch.
literas· apud
Scalig.de emend.
temp.l 5 p.496.
Spond.ad annum
302 n. 4.

drian martyr'd, but they put men to their oaths, to find out whether they were Chriſtians,that they might maſſacre them.

And in the 3^d, it was the like,when Miracles they ſay were not g yet ceaſt, yet ſure the greateſt was the conſtancy of Chriſtians in adhering to this book & patience in ſuffering for it. For they report the h ſands on the ſea ſhore almoſt as eaſy to be numbred as the Martyrs of that age; what by a *Valerian*, *Decius, Maximinus* and *Severus,* but eſpeciall y by b *Diocleſian,* who put ſo many men to death for not delivering up their Bibles to be burnt, and refuſing to Sacrifice to his Gods, as if he meant to have depopulated the whole earth. And this is as notorious as that men do now profeſs that they are Chriſtians,and that theſe are holy Scriptures. Therefore I ſhall need to go no further.

Now among ſo many myriads who on the account of all theſe Miracles (whate're they were) ſuffer'd themſelves to be converted to the faith of Chriſt, and then as if they car'd for nothing but Religion and their Bibles, for them bore the loſs of goods, and life it ſelf, and engag'd their poſterity to do ſo alſo; that not one of theſe ſhould know whether indeed any ſuch miracles were wrought,

wrought, if any were reftor'd to life or no : (for
if they knew, then they were true:)and that among
fo numberlefs a crow'd of teachers, who
by affuming to fpeak languages, raife the dead,
work figns, drew in thofe Myriads to Religion
and the ftake, and went before them, gave them
an example both in faith and death; that not one
of all thofe fhould believe either the Miracles or
himfelf that did them: for if any one that did them
did believe them, fince he knew who did them,
they muft needs be certain : but not one of them
to know it, fure is fuch a thing as neither could
be don nor be imagin'd.

He therefore that requires ftrict evidence in
things of faith which cannot bear it, he that calls
for Mathematical demonftration, nor will believe
on eafier terms, yet is fo credulous and fo unwa-
ry,that he can believe fo many things which by the
nature and the difpofition of mankind I have demonftrated not poffible, which yet muft be true,
unlefs thefe fcriptures be from God : 'tis plain
he does not feek for certainty, but for a pretence
of not believing; would fain have his Infidelity
and Atheifm look more excufable, and is not fit
to be difputed with but to be exploded.

E

But

But if thefe fcriptures be from God, then whatfoever they affirm (with modefty I may conclude)
is true. And therfore when S*t* *Luke Acts.* 1. 1. de-
clares his *former treatife contain'd all that Jefus began both to do and teach until the day in which he was
taken up:* fince Chrift before he did afcend taught
every thing that was requir'd to be believ'd and
don in order to falvation, and more too ; therfore if his Gofpel did contain all that he taught,
and did, fince it did not contain all abfo-
lutly, it muft needs mean it contained all that
was neceffary, or it muft mean nothing. And fince
the fame S*t* *Luke* in the beginning of that Gofpel
does affirm he wrot it, that *Theophilus might know
the certainty of thofe things wherein he had bin inftru-
ed*; Tis plain he avers that the certain knowledg of all thofe things wherein the having bin
inftructed made *Theophilus* a Chriftian, might be
had out of that Gofpel: and when S*t* *Paul* fays
here, that *the Holy Scriptures are able to make us wife
unto falvation* through faith which is in *Chrift Jefus*, and S*t* John in his 20 chap. v. 31. *that tho he
had not wrot all the things that Jefus did, yet thofe
that he had wrot were written, that we might believe
that Jefus was the Chrift the fon of God, and that believing*

Luc. 1. 4)

lieving we might have life through his name ; Tis e-
vident the Scriptures fay that what was written
was fufficient to work that belief which was fufficient to life and falvation , as far as the *credenda*
do concur to it. And when St *Paul* in that verfe
that fucceeds my text, in moſt exprefs particular
words fets down the ufefullnefs of Scripture in
each feveral duty of a *man of God,* or preacher of
the Gofpel,both ſfor *Doctrine* of faith, for *reproof*
or *correction* of manners, and *inſtruction unto righ-
teoufnefs*, and tells you Gods exprefs end in in-
fpiring it, and confequently its ability when ſo
infpir'd was, *that the man of God might be made perfect,* throughly *furnisht unto every good work* that be-
longs to his whole office ; tis moſt certain that
what is fufficient for that office to *inſtruct,reprove,
correct* and *teach* in , muſt needs be fufficient to
believe and *practiſe* in for all men : *i. e.* what my
text affirms, they *are able to make us wiſe unto
falvation.*

I might call in Tradition univerfal to bear witnefs to this truth for holy Scriptures, if having
once demonſtrated that they are Gods word,
when that does affirm it, and bears witnefs to
it , there were need of any other. And this I dare
boldly

boldly fay, that if the Scripture did fay as exprefly, that the Pope had a fupremacy or foveragni-
ty over the whole Church, or that he or the Roman Church were infallible; their definition,
or the living voice of their prefent Church, a
moft fure rule of Faith, as it does fay Scripture
is able to make us wife unto falvation, thofe Articles
would fuffer no difpute, it would be blafphemy
or facriledg to limit or explain them by diftincti-
ons, when thofe fayings of the perfectnefs of
Scriptures are forc't to bear many. Then we
fhould have no complaints of the obfcurity of
thofe books; if thofe articles were either in the
Greek or Hebrew, they would never fay the
Bible were not fit to be a Rule of Faith, becaufe
the Language were unknown to the unlearned,
and they could not be infallibly fecure of the Tranf-
lation; were they there they would account them
fure enough, who think them plain enough al-
ready there, and that we muft believe them becaufe, *Thou art Peter, Feed my fheep,* and *Tell the
Church,* are there.

And for him that fhall affirm, all neceffaries
that muft make us *wife unto falvation* are not in
the Scripture, 'tis impoffible to give a rational account

count how it fhould come to pafs that fome are
there,the reft are not.

It muft be either on defign, or elfe by chance.
Now 1. That God fhould defign, when very many things that were not neceffary were to be written , that the main and fundamental ones fhould
be omitted : and when of the neceffaries moft
he did defign for Scripture , then He fhould not
fufferthe Apoftles to write the remainder of them:
and yet what he would not fuffer them to write ,
defign'd that the Trent Fathers (who I hope
have perfeƈted the Catalogue) fhould write all:
of thefe fince 'tis not poffible to give a reafon ,
'tis not therfore rational to affirm it was upon
defign. But

2. If he fhall fay it only happen'd fo by chance,
he does affront both Scriptures , and Gods Holy Spirit, who , as they affirm, infpir'd them for
this very end, to bring men to the faith and to falvation. But there is no place for chance in thofe
things that are don in order to an end , by the
defign, impulfe and motion ofthe infinit wifdom
of Gods holy Spirit. He certainly does moft un-
worthily reproch his Maker, who can think it
poffible, that what he did defign exprefsly and on

E 3   that

that account alone to attain fuch an end by(namely that men fhould believe and be fav'd) and in-
fpire it for that purpofe, fhould yet fail, not be
fufficient for that purpofe. And fure if it be fufficient it contains all neceffaries, otherwife it were
deficient in the main ; yea fo clearly alfo, as that
they,for whofe falvation they are intended, may
with ufe of fuch methods,as are obvious and agreed
upon by all men, underftand them : for otherwife
they could not be fufficient;if men could not be inftructed by them in things neceffary both to faith
and life,they could not *make them wife unto falvation.*

I muft confefs the Scripture labors under a great
prejudice againft this doctrine, from the different
fenfes and interpretations that are made of it, e-
ven in the moft fundamental points, by them that
grant it is the word of God ; when yet all ufe the
fame means to find out the meaning, and no
doubt they feek fincerely after it. But yet I think it
evident this happens not from the obfcurity of
Scripture, fince it is not only in the moft exprefs
texts; but alfo if you fhould fuppofe the doctrins
were as plain fet down there as words can exprefs
them, yet there are fuch principles affum'd into
the faith of different fects, as muft oblige them

to

to interpret diverfly the fame plain words. I am
not fo vain as to imagin that no places are obfcure
in Scripture , and I know that learned men have
arts by obfcure places to confound the plaineft,
juft as the Philofopher did motion. Neither am I
fo perverfe and fingular not to think that univerfal practife and profeffion of the Church does
much affure and confirm explications of Scriptures , whether obfcure or plain. But this I fay,
that the diverfities of explication come, as I now
faid, from the diverfity of principles or rather pre-
judices, and that this only is the caufe of it I thus
demonftrate.

Firft in the *Socinian,* who interprets all thofe
Scriptures , which the Catholic world hath ftill
apply'd to the Divinity and fatisfaction of Chrift,
that I name no more points, otherwife then the
Church did alway; and I affirm he does it,not becaufe he thinks the words do favor his interpretation, but becaufe his principle requires it; namely this, To admit nothing into his faith but what
agrees with that which he counts reafon , which
in a *Socinians* faith is judg of all points in the laft
refort. And I mean reafon upon natural principles, and thus I prove it. *Socinus* fpeaking of
Chrift's

Chrift's fatisfaction, fays the word is not in Scri-
*Ego quidem e-
tiam;fi non femel
fed fæpe id in
facris m:ni men-
tis fcriptum ex-
taret,non idcir-
co tamen ita rem
prorfus fe habe-
re crederem. So-
cin. de Jefu
Chr. Servatore
parte 3 c. 6 ope-
rum tom. 2. p.
204.*
pture, [a] yet if it were there very often I would not
believe it, becaufe it does not confift with right
reafon, that is with the arguments that he had
brought againft it drawn-from human principles.
And therefore he there adds; thofe things which
'tis apparent cannot be, (*i. e.* that appear fuch
to him who judges by the principles of natural
reafon, which yet cannot judg of fupernatural and
infinite beings,) tho the Holy Scripture does exprefly fay they are, yet muft not be admitted; *&*
idcirco facra verba in alium fenfum quam ipfa fonant per
inufitatos etiam tropos quandoq; explicantur: aud for
this reafon we make ufe of even unufual tropes,
ftrain'd figures to explain the words of Holy writ
to other fenfes then the words themfelves import.
And fo he therfore ferves that great variety of
words by which the Scripture does exprefs Chrifts
fuffering *for our fins*, in our ftead, as our facri-
fice; againft the univerfal notions of thofe words,
not only which the Church of Chrift, but which
the Jew's and which the heathen world had of
them. And when his reafon told him that Chrift
could not be *God one with his Father*, that he was
fo far from having any being from eternity, as
that

that he was not at all, till he had a being from the
Bleſſed Virgin ; Therfore when the Scripture faies
directly [a] *I and the Father are one* , he muſt ſtrain it
to this meaning , are of one mind , we agree in
one : altho Sᵗ *John* avert that, by [b] diſtinguiſhing
thoſe two expreſsly. Yea worſe, when to prove
that Chriſt had a being e're the world was made,
we urge from the firſt Chap. to the [c] *Hebr.* what
Sᵗ *Paul* produces from the [d] *Pſalms*, and does apply to him moſt particularly. *Thou Lord in the
beginning haſt lai'd the foundation of the earth , and
the Heavens are the works of thine hands ; they ſhall pe-
riſh , but thou remaineſt, and they all ſhall wax old as
does a garment ; and as a veſture ſhalt thou fold them
up , and they ſhall be changed : but thou art the ſame,
and thy years ſhall not fail.* They explain it thus :
that God by Chriſt will at laſt deſtroy theſe Heavens , and this Earth , and change them , according to that ſaying in the Pſalms; which altho the
Apoſtle produce at length , as it ſtood there, both
concerning the *Creation* and *deſtruction* of the
world, yet he intended only to apply this laſt to
Chriſt. And tho he ſay as well of the ſame Lord,
*Thou Lord in the beginning didſt lay the foundation of
the earth, and the heavens are the works of thine hands,*

John 10. 30.

[b] *Joh. 5. 7. The
Father the Word,
and the Holy
Ghoſt, and theſe
three are one. 8.
the Spirit, and
the Water and
the Blood, and
theſe three agree
in one.*
[c] *Heb. 1. 10. 11.
12.*
[d] *Pſal. 102. 25.
26. 27.*

as, *thou shalt change them* ; yet he meant no more
but that this change God would effect by Chrift.
It is not poffible that the text can give any the
leaft countenance to this interpretation. The different explication of this Scripture does not come
from the obfcurity of any words in it ; for in
the *Pfalm* they and we underftand the fame words
in the fame fenfe exactly : therfore that we
differ here,is not from any thing in the words quo-
ted, but is wholly from the Principle. And we
may not wonder, for the plain fenfe will not fute
with their Hypothefis.

There are no other that are inftanc'd in as dif-
fering from us in points of faith but the Romanifts. I know not whether they account thofe
differences to be in things neceffary to falvation.
*If that be true that they allow (for what caufe
they know beft,) fome that are reconcil'd to their
Church to communicate with ours , that is, join
in our worfhip , and by doing fo own the profeffion of our faith in diftinction to that of others, or
at leaft efpoufe the fcandal of the owning it; Then
one would think they muft account that there is
nothing in our worfhip don that is unlawful, nor
omitted that is neceffary , nor any thing Hereti-
cal

*The reafonable-
nefs of this fup-
pofition might
be demonftrated
if there were
any need of it.*

cal profeft, at leaft that there's no fcandal in the
owning that profeffion. For if there were, they
did allow them only to profefs and act grofs fin,
which certainly they would not do. So that poor
Proteftants when they are pleas'd to give leave may
be no Heretics, and therfore there is nothing of
it felf in that profeffion faulty. But yet on the o-
ther fide fince we fee they call us Heretics, and
when they have no power over us, damn us to Hell
fires, and when they have had power, damn'd us to
the fire and fagot alfo; fure they think the differences to be in things neceffary. But yet the account is eafy, how not the obfcurity of Scripture,
but a Principle or prejudice does caufe this. For
We are bound in confcience to grant they believe
their own Principles. Now 'tis a Principle with
them, that their Church cannot erre, and therfore
that their prefent faith and confequent depending
practife was their faith and practife alwaies. That it
may appear fo, they muft feek for countenance
from Scripture: and if any thing there feem to
thwart their faith or practife, they muft fmooth and
difguife it, that it may look friendly. And 'tis
moft certain if the Scripture fhould be never fo
exprefs againft them, whilft they think it is not

poffible

poffible that they can err, they cannot think it poffible Scripture can mean what it pretends to fpeak. Twere eafy to make inftances. As firft for invocation of the Saints departed, which with them is a point of faith, [a] *Bellar.* and *Cochleus* produce that of the Pfalms., *I will lift up mine eyes unto the hills from whence cometh my help.* Pfalm. 121. 1. and altho the text directs that looking up exprefsly to the *Lord that made heaven and earth.* v. 2. and tho it be a Principle with them, that on thofe everlafting hills there were no Saints in *Davids* time that could be invocated, they were all in *limbo* then they fay ; yet as I faid, they would have countenance from Scripture, and for want of better they are therefore forc'd to interpret thofe words, *I will lift up mine eys unto the Hills,* thus, *I will invocate* the Saints. Now will any fay 'tis the obfcurity of this Scripture that does hinder Proteftants from feeing the bright evidence of this argument, and not rather that it is the weak foundation of this practice that does make the Romanifts feek to build it on thofe mountains? So among thofe feveral texts which in the 2d Nicen general Council are produc't for adoration of the images of Chrift and of the Saints, and are expounded to

evince

[a] *L. 1. de Sanct. Beatit. c. 17.*

evince it, none is plainer then that which I pro-
duced now from Bellarmin. I fhall give one or
two examples from the Pfalms : ^a*Thy face Lord* [a] Pfal. 27. 8. [b] Pfal. 4. 6.
will I feek: ^band, *Lord lift thou up the light of thy
countenance upon us :* and again, ^c*the rich among the* [c] Pfal. 45.12.
*people fhall entreat thy face:*therefore David thought
the picture of Chrift was to be ador'd. It is their
own ^d conclufion from thefe texts, And they have [d] *Concil tom* 18. p. 295.
no better for it. Yet they faw the doctrine in thefe
fo apparently, as that with great oppofition to
great Councils, and more blood fhed I think
then yet ever any doctrine hath bin fetled with,
it was impos'd. Yea more,the firft experiment of
the Popes power over Soveraign Princes was on
the account of this fame doctrine: when for op-
pofing Image-worfhip *Gregory the* 2^dexcommunica-
ted the Greek Emperour. Pope *Constantine* for the [*] *Sigon. de reg-no Ital. ad an-num* 712.*l.*3. *p.* 94.
fame caufe indeed had 14 years before don fo to
Philippicus, but he did not go much further,where-
as *Gregory* abfolv'd theEmperors fubjects in the Ro-
manDutchy fromtheirAllegiance;commanded them [a] *Sigon. de regno Ital. ad annum.* 726.*l.*3.*p.*103.
not to pay him any tribute,nor in any wife obey him; [b] *Leonis impe-rium refpue-runt, ac folen*
whereupon they ^akill'd their Governors,and ^bfwore

o

ni facramento fe Pontificis vitam ftatumq; in perpetuum defenfuros, atque ejus in omnibus rebus autori.
tati obtemperaturos jurarunt. Ita Roma Romanufq; ducatus à Græcis ad Romanum Pontificem pervenit.Sigon
de Regno Ital. ad. annum 727. l. 3. p. 105.

obedience

obedience to the Pope. And this was the beginning of St Peters patrimony, and it was thus gotten
by this doctrine, which they saw so cleerly in
these Scriptures; when they cannot see the contrary in those plain words; *Thou shalt not make to
thy self any* whether *Graven image* or idol it matters
not, since it follows, *nor the likeness of any thing
which is in heaven above,* &c. nor in those where
God takes care expresly that himself be not wor-
ship't by an image *Deut.* 4.·15. and then judg if
'tis obscurity or plainness that makes them see or
not see doctrines in the Scripture: rather if it be
not meerly the necessity of prejudice. So again
we differ in the meaning of the 14th chap. of the
1. *Cor.* where we think St *Paul* asserts and argues,
yea and chides against all service in an unknown
tongue in the public assemblies, saying all must
be don there so as it may be ^{c} understood, and to
edification. But that which is perform'd there in
an unknown tongue does not ^{d} edify says he there:
yet to justify this practice they must make it have
a different meaning, which no Fathers countenance, but which * several expound as we do, yea

^{c} 1 Cor. 1. 5.
12. 19. 2c.
^{d} V.6.14.16. 17.

*Basil. Mag. in
reg. brevior. in-
terrog. 278.
Tom.2.p.641.

Theodor.& Cecumen. in locum &c. and the commentary under St *Ambros*'s name makes these who in
the Church of Corinth would use an unknown tongue in their sacred offices,(against whom St *Paul*
directs his speech,and takes occasion for that which he saies in this chap.)converted Hebrew's; who
would it should seem perform the service or at least some parts of it in the Christian Assemblies,
as they had bin don of old in the Synagogues,in the Hebrew tongue,which the Corinthians understood not, against which St. *Paul* disputes.   and

and diverſe of their own do ſo too, and particu-
larly their Pope *John* 8th in his 247th Epiſtle
writing expreſly on that Subject. Once more, ſo
their half communion, that it may be reconcil'd
with that expreſs command [b] *Drink yee all of it*: and
this do, obliges them to find another meaning:
drink ye all muſt be directed to them only as A-
poſtles; and *do this* muſt ſignify conſecrate the
Elements, altho St *Paul* apply it moſt directly to
the drinking, and the drinking to his lay Corinthians. Nor dare they ſay in truth it means the
other, for St *Paul* when he does ſay *do this*, did not
intend to make his *Lay Corinthians* male and female
all [c] prieſts, and give them power to conſecrate. The
words are plain, ther's nothing in the text obſcure
that makes us differ; but the practiſe had by little
& little grown upon them, till it became Univerſal,
and ſo grew into their faith: and then ſince they
believe they cannot erre, they muſt expound
Chriſt's words ſo as they may not contradict
their practiſe; becauſe that would overthrow
their Principle.

But the Church that builds upon no Principle
but Cods word, can have no temtation to pervert
or ſtrain it, ſince what ever does appear to be the
meaning

[a] Conc. tom. 24. p. 287.

[b] Mat. 26.27.

1 Cor. 11.25.

[c] Yet the Counc. of Trent Seſſ.22. c.9. can. 2. pronounces Anathe-ma to all thoſe that ſhall ſay theſe words do this, quoting them alſo in the margin out of this place 1 Cor. 11 did not conſtitute preiſts, and ordain that they ſhould offer the body and blood of Chriſt. Edit Col.Agrip. anno 1261.

meaning of it, that their Principle muſt needs engage them to believe. And therfore if it ſay *This is
my body*, we believe it; if it ſaies too after conſe-
cration it is ᵃ *bread*, we believe that alſo: and becauſe it therfore ſays 'tis both, we ſo believe it
one that it may be the other : which ſince both
ſay it is impoſſible that it can be ſubſtantially,
neither hath God in exprefs words told us which
it is ſubſtantially; therfore ſeeing when he calls it
body, he is inſtituting his *Sacrament*, there's all
reaſon in the world he ſhould mean *Sacramental-
ly* ; ſince 'tis the moſt proper meaning : and by
conſequence 'tis bread *ſubſtantially*, as all waies of
judging in the world aſſure us. Here's no ſtreſs
on Scripture, as there is no Principle to ſerve ;
when as the other makes us differ, not in Scripture only, even where 'tis plaineſt ; but tradition too. For the moſt exprefs and evident ſay-
ings of the primitive Fathers are on every head of
difference, as much the matter of contention as
the texts of Scripture are ; as it were eaſy to de-
monſtrate if that were my buſineſs. So that it is meer
deceit to lay our quarrels to defects in Gods
word, and particularly to its obſcurity, which
a man would think were evident enough from
this

this that *Children knew it.* The laft thing I am to
fpeak to.

*And that from a child thou haft known the holy
Scriptures, which are able to make thee wife unto falvation through faith which is in Chrift Jefus.*

I cannot pafs this, that it is St *Chryfoftomes* ob-
fervation, that *Timothy* was nurft up in the Scriptures from his childhood. Yea and fince his Father was an Heathen, he muft have bin taught them
by his *Grandmother Loïs* , and *his Mother Eunice* ,
whofe faith St *Paul* fpeaks of 2 *Tim.* 1. 5. *Children* therfore then , and *Women* , and they fure are
Laics , read the Bible. Yea and fince they knew
it, they muft read it in a language which they
underftood : and we know where that is unlawful now. If we confider the firft prohibition that
appear'd in that Church with Synodical autority
againft fuch mens having any Bibles in their own
tongue , we fhall find it was immediately upon
the preaching of the *Waldenfes* , one of whofe
doctrines it was,[a] *that the Scripture was the rule to
judg of faith by* : *fo that whatfoever was not confonant
to that muft be refus'd.* This they preach't in France
and over Europe in the latter end of the[b] 12 Cen-

G   tury :

.*Uffer. de Chrif.*
Eccle. fucceff.
c. 6. §. 17.

b *c.* 8. §. 1.

*Spicileg. tom.
2. p. 624.*

tury; and that Council which forbad their having of the Bible, we find lately put forth by the
frier ^c D. Achery as held at *Tholoufe* in the beginning of the 13th Century. It feems they apprehen-
ded then their doctrines hardly would abide that
touchftone: And they therfore had no furer, more
compendious way for its fecurity then to prevent
fuch trial, taking care men fhould not know what
was or what was not in Scripture. And it is not
poffible for me to give account why in their ca-
techifing they leave out all that part of the com-
mandments, *Thou fhalt not make to thy felf any graven
image,* &c. but this only, that they dare not let the
laity compare their doctrine and their practice
with that Scripture. But tho it is poffible they
might conceive fome danger if the whole Scripture fhould be expos'd, yet in thofe portions
which the Church it felf chofe out for her own offices, the *little leffons,* and *Epiftles,* and *Gofpels,*
thofe fure one would think were fafe: no, not their
*Pfalter, Breviary,*nor their *Hours of the Bleffed Virgin*
muft they have tranflated in their own tongue;

cap. 4.

as that ^a Council did determin. And truly when
the Roman Miffal was turn'd lately into French,
and had bin allow'd to be fo by the general Affembly

bly of the Clergy in the year [a] 1650. and when it was don it had the usual approbation of the Doctors and some Bishops, and then was printed at Paris with the licenfe of the Vicars general of their Archbishop. Yet another general assembly of the Clergy the year 1660, whereat there were [b] 36 Bishops, upon pain of [c] excommunication forbid any one to read it, and condemn not only that prefent traduction, but the thing in general as [d] poyfonous, in an Encyclical Epistle to all the Prelates of the Kingdom : and in [e] another they say of him that did translate it, and the vicars general that did defend him in it, that by doing fo *they did take armes against the Church, attaquing their own Mother* (namely by that verfion) *at the Altar, in that fanctuary, that clofet of her fpoufes myfteries to proftitute them* : and in another Epistle they befeech his Holinefs Pope *Alexander* 7th to damn it not in France alone but the whole Church; which he then did by his [g] Bull, for ever interdicting that or any other verfion of that book, [h] for-

Marginal notes:

[a] *Ordonnance de Meßieurs les Vicaires Generaux de Monfeigneur l'Eminentiſſime Cardinal de Retz Archeveſque de Paris, which is in the* 137th *page of the Extrait du Procez verbal de l' Aſſemblée general du Clergé de France, tenuë à Paris en l'année 1660.*

[b] *p.* 128 *of that extrait.*

[c] *Ibid. p.* 128.

& p. 139.

[d] *p.* 130.

*ep.*141.*les enfans de noſtre mere ont pris les armes contre nous, ils la vont attaquer jufques dans le Sanctuaire, des Myſteres de fon Efpoux pour les proſtituer.*

[f] *p.* 132.

[g] *p.* 147 *and the fame bull is printed in the Index of prohibited books fet out by the command of Alex.* 7. *at Rome* 1664. *p.* 382.

[h] *Miſſa le præfatum Gallico idiomate confcriptum vel in poſterum alias quomodolibet confcribendum & exulgandum perpetuo damnamus, reprobamus, & interdicimus, ejufque impreſſionem, lectionem & retentionem univerſis & fingulis utriufque fexus Chrifti fidelibus, cujufcunque gradus, ordinis, conditionis exiſtant, fub pæna excommunicationis latæ fententiæ ipfo jure incurrendæ perpetuo prohibemus : mandantes quod ſtatim quicunque illud habuerint, vel in futurum quodcunque habebunt realiter & cum effectu exhibeant & tradant locorum Ordinariis vel inquifitoribus, qui nulla interpofita mora, exemplaria igne combirant, & comburi faciant.*

bidding

bidding all to read or keep it on feverest paines;
commanding any one that had it to deliver it immediately to the Inquifitor or Ordinary that
it might be burnt forthwith. Now thus (whatever it be otherwife) the mafs is certainly a fa-
crifice when 'tis made a burnt offering to ap-
peafe his holinefs's indignation : when that very Memorial of Chrifts paffion again fuffers, and
their facred offices are martyr'd. To fee the difference of times; 'twas heretofore a *Pagan Dio-
clefian*, a ftrange prodigy of cruelty, who by his
edict did command all Chriftians to deliver up their
Bibles or their bodies to be burnt : 'Twas here
his *Holinefs*, *Chrifts Vicar*, who by his Bull or-
ders all to give up theirs, that is all of it that they
will allow them, and their praiers alfo, that
they may be forthwith burnt, or themfelves to
be excommunicated, that is their fouls to be de-
voted to eternal flames. And whereas then thofe
only that did give theirs up were excommuni-
cate, all Chriftians fhun'd them as they would
the plague; and multitudes, whole regions rather gave themfelves up to the fire to preferve their
Bibles : now thofe only that have none, or that
deliver up theirs, are the true obedient fons of
                                                      that

that Church, and the thorough Catholics. I know
men plead great danger in that book: it is repre-
fented as the fource of monftrous doctrines and
rebellions. I will not fay thefe men are bold that
take upon them to be wifer then Allmighty God,
and to fee dangers he forefaw not, and to prevent them by fuch methods as thwart his ap-
pointments ; but I will fay that thofe who talk thus
certainly defpife their hearers; as if we knew not
Herefies were hatcht by thofe that underftood the
Bible untranflated : and as if we never heard there
were rebellions among them that were forbid to
read the Bible. For if there were a *Covenant* a-
mong them that had it in their own tongue, fo
there was an *Holy League* amongft thofe men that
were deni'd it. While thofe that had the guidance
of the fubjects confcience were themfelves fubject
to a forreign power, as all Priefts of that communion are, How many Kings and Emperors
have there bin that did keep the Scriptures from
their people, but yet could not keep their people
from fedition, nor themfelves from ruine by it ? In
fine when God himfelf for his own people caus'd
his Scripture to be written in their own tongue,
to be weekly read in public to, and day and night

in private by the people ; and when the Apoſtles by the inſpiration of the *Holy Ghoſt* indited Scripture for the world, they did it in the language that was then moſt vulgar to the world : what *God* and the *Holy Spirit* thus appointed as the fitteſt means for the Salvation of the world, to define not expedient, as the Holy Fathers of *Trent* did, looks like blaſphemy againſt *God* and the *Holy Spirit*. But blaſphemies of this kind are not to be wonder'd at from that kind of men, that call the Scripture a *dumb* [a]*judg,* [b]*a black Goſpel,* *incken Divinity,* [c]*written not that they ſhould be the rule of our faith and Religion, but that they ſhould be regulated by, ſubmitted to our faith;* [d]*that the autority of the Church hath given canonical autority to Scriptures, and thoſe the chief, which otherwiſe they had not neither from themſelves nor from their authors;* And *that if the Scriptures were not ſuſtain'd by the autority of the Church they would be of no more value then Æſops* [e]*fables.* [f]*And laſtly, that the people are permitted to read the bible was the invention of the Devil.*

But to leave the controverſy and ſpeak to the advantages which may be had from early inſtitution in the Scripture ; 'tis ſo evident that I need not

[a] *Pigh.* 3. *de hier. Ecc.*
[b] *Eccius.*
[c] *Pigh. de hier. l.1.c.2. fol.* 8.
[d] *Idem Pigh.*

[e] *Vid.Chemn. examen de S. Can. p.* 47.
[f] *Peres. de tradit.par.1.aſſert.* 3.

not obferve how 'tis for want of principles impreft
and wrought into the mind in Childhood, that our
youth is fo licencious. And 'tis not pofiible it
can be otherwife, when they have nothing to op-
pofe to conftitution, when tis growing, and to
all the temtations both of objects and example;
no ftrict fenfe of duty planted in them, no fuch
notions as would make refiftance to the rifings
of their inclination, and feducements of ill company: and they therefore follow and indulge to all
of them. And in Gods name why do parents
give their Children up to God in their firft infancy, deliver him fo early a poffeffion of them? as
if they would have Religion to take feizure on
them ftrait, as if by their baptizing them fo foon,
they meant to confecrate their whole lives to Gods
fervice, make them his as foon as they were theirs,
as if they had bin given them meerly for Gods u-
fes? And they therfore enter them into a vow of
Religion almoft as foon as they have them: why
all this? if accordingly they do not feafon and
prepare them as they fhall grow capable. Why
when they are but newly born their children, do
they take care they fhall be regenerate and born
again Gods children? if they do not furnifh them
with

with neceffaries, educate them into all the qua-
lities and hopes that appertain to the condition
of Gods children , as well as they do to that of
their own. That parent which not only, like
fome delicate ones refufes her own breafts to her
own infant, but provides no other to fuftain it;
that does only wafh her babe from i'ts firft blood
and uncleannefs to expofe it the more handfom
prey to wolves and tigers in the defert, is more
favage then thofe tigers:[a] *even the fea monfters draw*
out the breafts ; they give fuck to their young ones ,
faith lamenting *Jeremy*, but he adds *the daughter*
of my people is cruel like the Oftrich in the wilder-
nefs , [b] *which leaveth her eggs in the earth, and for-*
getteth that the foot may crufh them, or that the
wild beaft may break them , fhee is hardned againft
her young ones : fuch are they who when their
children are fo born again to God, yet as they
fhall wax capable provide not that which St *Peter*
calls the *fincere milk of the word that they may grow*
thereby: but from their being wafht fo in the la-
ver of regeneration , take no more care, but expofe them forthwith to fuch lufts and converfati-
ons, as are much more wild and favage then thofe
beafts in the comparifon ; to which they cannot
choofe

[a] Lam. 4. 3.
[b] Job. 39. 14.
[c] 1 Pet. 2. 2.

choofe but be a prey. They ftrive indeed, they fay, to educate them into men betimes, that is, make them converfible and bold:and fince for that they muft engage them into frequent company, where they fee and hear mens follies, that I fay no worfe; by that means they come to have their underftandings ftor'd with nothing but the Modes, and fins of converfation ; fill'd with froth and puddle; men betimes only thus, as they have forwarded their inclinations to, and got an early underftanding and experience of, thofe vices, which one would think men only could be equal for. But by this means the mind, that only part that makes us be men, is not only not improv'd, but dwarft. They do not only ftill continue children in their underftanding,as to any thing that's real and folid; but the hopes of reafon are deftroy'd in them, and its growth kill'd, by turning all its nurifh-ment to feed the beaft part ; and the Chriftian is quite ftarv'd. There needs no other caufe be given for the moft part, why fo many men have no Religion, own being Libertines, and profefs vice; for want of education they have nothing in them that does check this, for they had no principles of a Religion inftil'd into them. And if at any time

H   it

it comes to pafs that they think it is their inte-
reft to take upon them the profeffion of fome Religion, they therfore, fince they have no Principles nor rules to judg by, are moft apt to choofe
to profefs that Religion, which is like to be moft
gentle to the courfes they have fteer'd, and are
engag'd in. Now that men hope to find fuch an
one, (whether by its conftitution I fhall not en-
quire but,) by i'ts practice is but too appaernt. Accordingly when they go over to it, they carry with
them, and preferve in it the vices of their no Religion; and by confequence they went not over
ferioufly for Religion: and are therfore fo much
worfe now then when they own'd no Religion,
that they do their wickedneffes with certainty of
eafy abfolution, and fo hopes of falvation; and
by this are likely to be made twofold more children of Hell then before: and let them triumph
in fuch conquefts. Ther's nothing in the world
that contributes fo much to this as mens being not
acquainted early with, inftructed in, thofe divine
rules and obligations to piety and virtue, which
this book the Bible does afford. If men had bin
feafon'd firft with the knowledg and the fenfe of
duty, with the comforts that are in it, with the

appre-

apprehenfions of great bleffings that attend it;and
the mifchiefs that are confequent, indeed effenti-
al to impiety and vice here; and their minds were
furnifht with examples of both, which this book
abounds with; and their hearts too rais'd with
expectations of far greater bleffednefs in a life here-
after, and with the belief that both that bleffednefs and life fhall have no end : and were made
fenfible alfo of ftrange dreadful torments that a-
wait the breach of duty, which fhall alfo laft for
ever : If thefe impreffions I fay, did prevent all o-
ther, and take up the mind, and had in them the
ftamp and character of *God*, and fo there were a
reverence and awe of him wrought in them, and
they lookt upon him as concern'd in all this; how
it was his word that faid it ; and thefe fentiments
were grown into the very habit of their mind; as
it would not be eafy to corrupt or foften fuch, fo
'twould be much more difficult to fhake them, fince
their faith is founded on *the rock of ages.* Befides the
Holy Scriptures carry in them fuch an obligation of
adhering to them, and to them alone, fince they are
fufficient *to make us wife unto falvation,* and are *Gods
word,* that men would not be apt to exchange them
for Legends,pious forgeries,for things that can make

good no certain title from the Lord: for let them
fhew an equal derivation of it, bring it down
through all the ages ae we have don the Scriptures
title to him. Otherwife it juftly may provoke Gods

• Jer. 2. 13.

exclamation in the Prophet ª " Jeremy : Be afto-
" nifht O ye Heavens, and be horribly afraid, be
" yee very defolate; faith the Lord, for my people
" have committed two evils, they have forfaken
" me the fountain of living waters, and hew'd
" them out cifterns, broken cifterns that can hold
" no water: cifterns therfore that may leave them
in a ftate to want a drop of water, when their
tongue fhall be horribly tormented : whereas he
that drinks that *living water* which Chrift gives,

ᵇ Joh. 4. 14.
compard with
c. 5. 34.

his ᵇ *word, fhall never thirft,* but it fhall be a well of
water in him fpringing up to everlafting life.

F I N I S.

www.ingramcontent.com/pod-product-compliance
Lightning Source LLC
Chambersburg PA
CBHW031804090426
42739CB00008B/1153